WACKY COMPARISONS

HOW BIG?

WACKY WAYS TO COMPARE SIZE

BY JESSICA GUNDERSON   ILLUSTRATED BY KEINO

How big is a GORILLA?
Or a GRIZZLY'S PAW?

Is either as big as a TARANTULA?

A manatee, an ostrich egg—
Look inside to see how big!

PICTURE WINDOW BOOKS
a capstone imprint

The mice exclaim, "THIS ISN'T FAIR!

583 of our PAWS equal 1 GRIZZLY BEAR'S."

1 bear paw = 35 square inches (226 square centimeters); 1 mouse paw = 0.06 sq. in. (0.4 sq cm)

Grizzly

24 large-sized **CHICKEN EGGS** weigh

as much as **1** **OSTRICH EGG**

hatching today!

1 ostrich egg = 3 pounds (1.4 kilograms); 1 chicken egg = 2 ounces (57 grams)

The **DOLPHIN** jumps through hoops and swims.

67,825 CANDIES fit inside him.

The **EMPIRE STATE BUILDING** is the same height as **284 GORILLAS** in the bright moonlight.

The **FERRIS WHEEL** is a giant ride.

36 CAR TIRES fit inside.

1 Ferris wheel = 63 ft. (19 m); 1 tire = 21 in. (53 centimeters)

1 TARANTULA looking for a meal

fits **15 PENNIES** on its back.

WHAT A DEAL!

1 spider = 6 sq. in. (39 sq cm); 1 penny = 0.4 sq. in. (2.6 sq cm)

A hot-air balloon floats toward the sun.

How many **BIRTHDAY BALLOONS** fit inside **1**?

154,000

64 MINI PRETZELS lined end to end are as long as **1** OCTOPUS ARM that won't bend.

PRETZELS

1 arm = 8 ft. (2.4 m); 1 pretzel = 1½ in. (3.8 cm)

How many RED BLOOD CELLS fit inside

1 MOSQUITO'S BELLY

that's satisfied?

1 meal = 0.0003 fluid ounces (0.01 milliliters or 10 microliters); 5 million red cells per microliter

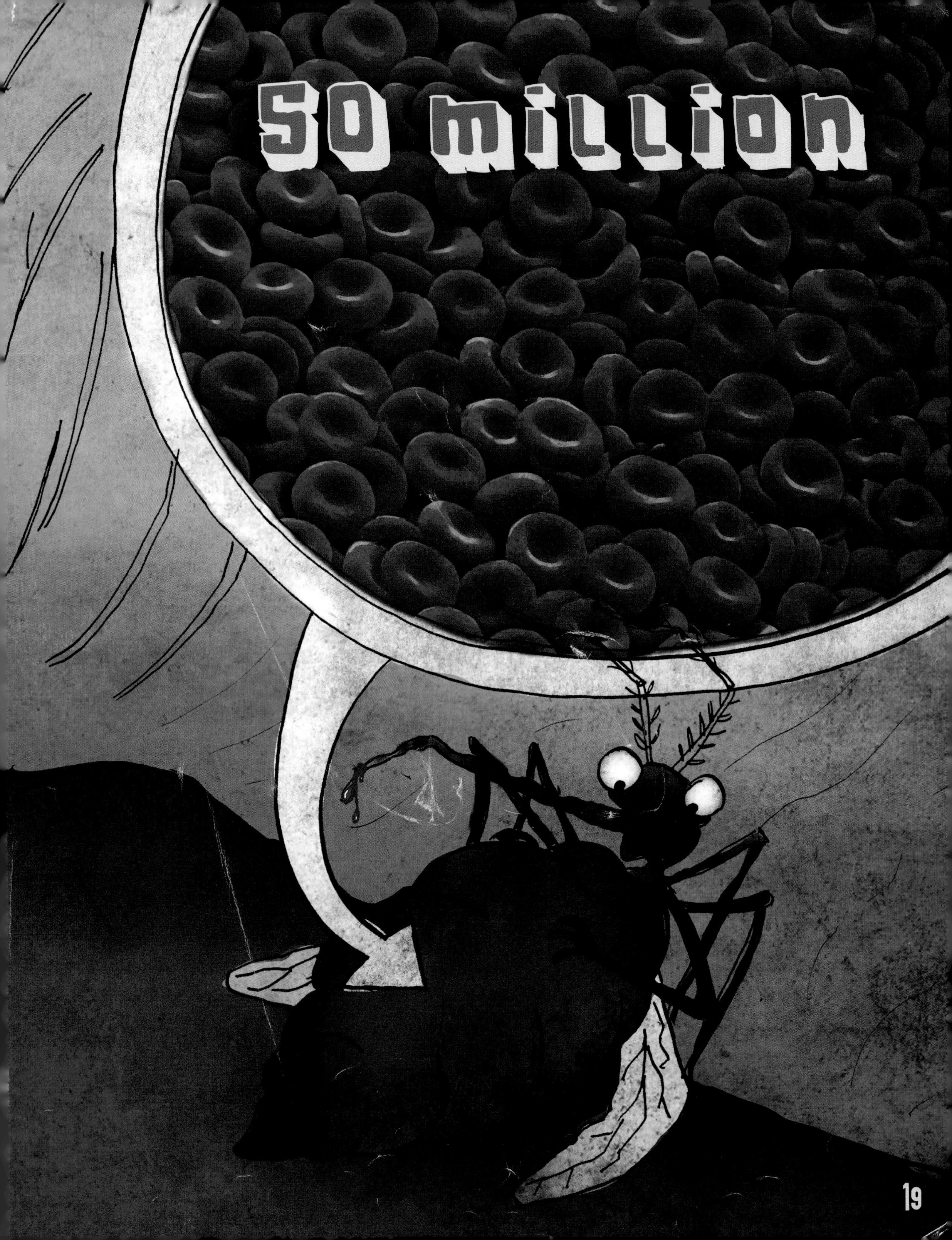
50 million

The NEWFOUNDLAND is a dog so great,
it takes **24** CHIHUAHUAS to match its weight.

1 Newfoundland = 145 lb. (66 kg); 1 Chihuahua = 6 lb. (2.7 kg)

1,226,880 PEAS
fit inside 1 MANATEE.

We've seen big apes
reach for the stars.

But now I wonder
HOW BIG **YOU** ARE!

1 manatee = 71 cu. ft. (2 cu m); 1 pea = 0.1 cu. in. (1.6 cu cm)

READ MORE

Accorsi. William. *How Big Is the Lion?: My First Book of Measuring.* Measure Me! New York: Workman Pub., 2010.

Coffelt. Nancy. *Big. Bigger. Biggest!* New York: Henry Holt and Co., 2009.

Nunn. Daniel. *Animals Big and Small.* Math Every Day. Chicago: Raintree, 2012.

INTERNET SITES

FactHound offers a safe, fun way to find Internet sites related to this book. All of the sites on FactHound have been researched by our staff.

Here's all you do:

Visit *www.facthound.com*

Type in this code: 9781404883253

Special thanks to our adviser, Terry Flaherty, PhD, Professor of English, Minnesota State University, Mankato, for his expertise.

Editor: Jill Kalz
Designer: Ashlee Suker
Art Director: Nathan Gassman
Production Specialist: Eric Manske
The illustrations in this book were created digitally.

Picture Window Books are published by Capstone,
1710 Roe Crest Drive, North Mankato, Minnesota 56003
www.capstonepub.com

Library of Congress Cataloging-in-Publication Data
Gunderson, Jessica.
  How big? : wacky ways to compare size / by Jessica Gunderson ; illustrated by Keino.
    pages cm. — (Wacky comparisons)
  Summary: "Compares various big objects to smaller objects in unique, illustrated ways"—Provided by publisher.
  Audience: K to grade 3.
  Includes bibliographical references.
  ISBN 978-1-4048-8325-3 (library binding)
  ISBN 978-1-4795-1915-6 (paperback)
  ISBN 978-1-4795-1911-8 (eBook PDF)
1. Size perception—Juvenile literature. 2. Comparison (Philosophy)—Juvenile literature. I. Keino, illustrator. II. Title.

BF299.S5G86 2014
530.8—dc23   2013012153

Printed in the United States of America in North Mankato, Minnesota.
032013   007223CGF13

LOOK FOR ALL THE BOOKS IN THE SERIES:

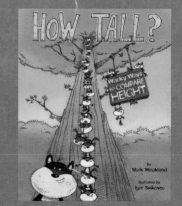